3 1994 01431 8502

SANTA ANA PUBLIC LIBRARY
NEWHOPE BRANCH

FIRST Budget SMARTS

J 332.024 PET
Peterson, Judy Monroe
First budget smarts

$29.25
NEW HOPE   31994014318502

Judy Monroe
Peterson

ROSEN
PUBLISHING®

New York

To Nick, for all your good advice

Published in 2010 by The Rosen Publishing Group, Inc.
29 East 21st Street, New York, NY 10010

Copyright © 2010 by The Rosen Publishing Group, Inc.

First Edition

All rights reserved. No part of this book may be reproduced in any form without permission in writing from the publisher, except by a reviewer.

Library of Congress Cataloging-in-Publication Data

Peterson, Judy Monroe.
First budget smarts / Judy Monroe Peterson.
    p. cm.—(Get smart with your money)
Includes bibliographical references and index.
ISBN-13: 978-1-4358-5273-0 (library binding)
ISBN-13: 978-1-4358-5552-6 (pbk)
ISBN-13: 978-1-4358-5553-3 (6 pack)
1. Budgets, Personal—Juvenile literature. 2. Young adults—Finance, Personal. I. Title.
HG179.P44724 2010
332.0240084'2—dc22

                                                            2008040549

Manufactured in Malaysia

Contents

Introduction

Perhaps you are saving money to buy a car. Your parents have told you that you must pay for part of the gas and the insurance. Now, you wonder if you will have enough money to pay for a car and these other costs.

Maybe you want to go to college. However, you do not know if you are saving enough money. You like to have fun, too. Your friends are planning to see a movie and then have pizza on Saturday night. You are short on cash, but you do not want to ask your parents or a friend for money. Then, you remember some cash that you had tucked in your desk drawer for an emergency. Should you use that money to go out on Saturday?

Knowing how to earn, spend, and save money are important money management skills. You can learn and practice these skills. Using good money management skills can help you become financially independent. These skills will also help you reach your goals in life.

Making and following a budget are key to managing your money. Budgeting helps you understand what you earn, how you spend it, and how you save it. By making a budget, you have a summary of your current

Some teens turn an interest or hobby into a business. Because she loves pets, this teen walks dogs for other people to earn money.

finances. You can then use this summary to make smart money choices. For example, you can determine if you have enough money to buy and operate a car, or to pay rent for an apartment, as well as the electricity. Using budgets can also help you reach larger goals, such as going to college.

You might have heard of people who do not make budgets or consider them too much work. Some people do not like making budgets. Others make budgets but do not stick to them. Have you ever heard someone say, "I just blew my budget!" after buying an expensive item?

Do you ever wonder where your money goes? Do you sometimes find that you cannot pay for the things you want? A budget takes the guesswork out of managing your money.

Good budgets include income, expenses, and savings. Income is any money that you receive from someone or money that you earn. Earnings are money you receive for doing work. Income is money coming in. Expenses are money going out.

You might get income in a variety of ways. You might earn wages from a part-time job. You might get an allowance from a parent or guardian for doing regular chores around the house. Sometimes, you might be paid to do special projects, such as cleaning the attic or garage, or helping someone move.

You might earn money by having a business that sells services, goods, or products. Services include babysitting, tutoring, mowing lawns, and walking dogs. Or, you might sell goods like handmade bird feeders or chopped firewood.

What do you do with your income? Do you spend all of your money as soon as you get it? Or, do you save part or all of your income? Do you hide your savings under the bed or put it into a savings account at a bank?

Proper budgeting can help you reach your money goals. Income, savings, and expenses affect personal money goals. In addition, your money goals might not be the same as your friend's money goals. You might be saving to buy a car, while your friend is saving for a new computer and printer. Both are examples of long-term goals because buying a new car or computer generally costs more than a weekly paycheck or monthly allowance. Making and following a budget can help you reach your short-term and long-term money goals. A budget gives you a picture of where your money is going now and where it might go in the future. Budgeting can help you save your money. You can adjust your budget as your financial needs change.

Without a budget, you might find yourself living from day to day. You might not have enough money for things you want now or even in the future. A budget will help you meet small goals, such as going to the movies with friends or buying new clothes. You can use your budget to help you plan for bigger goals, like buying a computer or car. You can also plan for even larger goals, such as paying for an education. When you take control of your money with a budget, you will feel more confident about your future.

CHAPTER 1

Your Weekly Income and Expense Records

reating a budget takes several steps. The first
step is to know your income and expenses.
Recall that income is any money you receive.
Expenses are whatever you spend your money on.

Sources of Income

Where do you get your income? Typical sources
of income include gifts. Family members and
friends might give you money for your birthday
or other special occasions.

Perhaps you earn some of the money that you
spend. You might get a paycheck by working
a job outside your home. Perhaps you work in a
grocery store as a cashier or bagger, or maybe
you work in a fast-food restaurant. When you
receive your paycheck, you will see the gross pay,
or the total amount earned before deductions
are subtracted. Deductions are amounts that are
withheld from, or taken out of, your gross pay.
These include federal income tax, Social Security
tax, and Medicare tax. Your state government
might require that state income tax be withheld.
The net pay is the amount of money you receive
after all deductions have been subtracted.

Income can come from part-time jobs. This teen works as a cashier at the checkout counter in a busy supermarket.

Average Weekly Income, Week of January 9–15

Paycheck, cashier job	$ 120.89
Odd job, snow shoveling	$ 10.00
Cash for birthday	$ 50.00
Cash from Dad	$ 20.00
Sold DVD	$ 5.00
Actual Total:	$ 205.89
Rounded Up:	$ 206.00

Making a Weekly Expense Record

The next step in making a budget is to know what you currently buy. You need to know how much money you spend to buy goods or services, or you could budget unrealistic amounts for your expenses. Keeping an expense record for a week will show you what you have bought for that week. In turn, knowing these expenses will help you make your budget.

Look at the sample of a weekly expense record on page 13. To make an expense record, set up a worksheet in a word processing or spreadsheet program. Or, use a notebook or sheets of paper clipped together. Enter the title "Expense Record" and the date. Then, make a table with three columns. Enter the date you bought an item, the name of the item, and the cost. Include any expenses that you pay for by cash, check, credit card, or debit card. Keep track of all your expenses, including gas, bus or subway fares, clothing, shoes, jewelry, soda and candy, tickets to a movie, and so on. Jot down everything, even if the amount is less than a dollar.

Ask for and keep receipts for anything that you buy. Use your receipts to help you remember what you bought as you keep your expense record. You might want to keep your receipts in a large envelope, folder, or small box.

Expense Record, Week of January 9-15

Monday

Lunch at school	$ 5.00
Soda	$ 2.00
Gas for car	$ 40.00
Haircut	$ 18.00

Tuesday

Magazine	$ 5.00
Gift for friend	$ 20.00
Gum and soda	$ 3.00
Music downloads	$ 3.00

Wednesday

Baseball cap	$ 15.00
Chips and soda	$ 3.00

Thursday

Music downloads	$ 5.00

Friday

Pizza, fries, shake	$ 18.00

Saturday

DVD rental	$ 8.00
Popcorn, soda	$ 8.00
Jacket	$ 76.00

Sunday

Music downloads	$ 5.00

Total:	**$234.00**

To help you keep track, fill out your expense record every time you buy something. Or, fill out your expense record two or three times each day. For example, you might want to fill in your expenses after lunch, after supper, and before going to bed. At the end of the week, add up your expenses and write the total. Round the money up to the nearest dollar.

Once you have your weekly expense record, look over your expenses and the total amount that you spent. Are you surprised at the total weekly cost for some of the items you bought, such as $13 in music downloads or $39 in food and snacks? Do you think you bought any unnecessary things? Did you borrow money from a friend or relative so that you could buy something?

Now, you want to know if your weekly expenses match your weekly income. Subtract the total of your weekly expenses from the total of your weekly income. In the sample on page 12, the weekly income was $206. In the sample on page 13, the expenses for the same week were $234. The person overspent by $28.

When you subtract your expenses from your income, you can have three results. If the difference is zero, then

All budgets have two parts: income (money in) and expenses (money out). To set up a budget, you first need to learn what your current expenses are.

Myths and Facts

Myth   Budgeting is difficult.

Fact   A budget is straightforward. When you budget, you use basic math: adding, subtracting, multiplying, and dividing. By budgeting, you take control of your own finances and decide your own financial goals. You will make your life happier and easier by avoiding the stress of living from day to day or with debt.

Myth   Very few people budget.

Fact   Many people and families create and follow budgets. You might not know this because people might not talk about their budgets. In addition, governments, federal agencies, businesses, and organizations prepare and manage budgets. Whether a budget is for one person or for many people, money must be managed carefully.

Myth   Having a budget is restrictive—it keeps a person from buying the things that he or she wants.

Fact   A budget is a spending plan. Think of your spending plan as a road map for your finances. Your budget will help you plan your finances now and for your future. A budget will show you what you can afford to spend on things that you want. A budget can also help you achieve your money goals.

you are balanced for that week. If the result is a positive number, then you have money left over. If your expenses are more than your income (a negative number or a minus sign), then you overspent. In all three cases, budgeting will help you manage your money now and in the future.

Keep your expense record for a second week or even longer. A monthly expense record will help you realize where your money is going. The more you see how you are spending your money, the easier it will be to manage your money.

Setting Up Categories

Look over your expenses again. In a word processing or spread-sheet file, or on a sheet of paper, write categories to group your expenses. Your categories might include transportation, eating out, snacks and soda, entertainment, clothes and shoes, school supplies, gifts, savings, and others.

Go over your categories for your weekly expense record. What categories did you spend the most on? Are you surprised at the totals for some categories? Can you think of categories you might have missed? Now that you have tracked your income sources and expenses for a week or more, you are ready to make your budget.

Chapter 2
Setting Up Your Monthly Budget

The purpose of budgeting is to find a balance between income and expenses. You want your income to be the same as or more than your expenses. You also want your budget to reflect your short-term and long-term financial goals.

Your budget will contain two sections: income and expenses. From your work in chapter 1, you already have a clear idea of what amounts make up your weekly income and expenses. Now, you will make a budget for a month. As you make your budget, you will add more information to both sections. Then, you will compare your income and expenses and evaluate your results.

Think of a budget as a table with two sections. Look at the budget template on page 22. The first section is "Net Income." The second section is "Expenses." Note the two types of expenses, fixed and variable. Fixed expenses stay the same from month to month. Rent is an example of a fixed expense. Variable expenses, such as food and entertainment, change over time.

You can set up your budget on a personal finance program or on a financial Web site. You can also use a word processing or

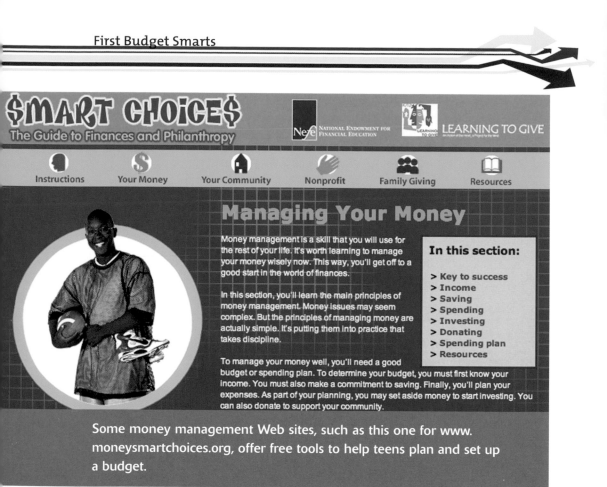

$MART CHOICE$
The Guide to Finances and Philanthropy

NEFE NATIONAL ENDOWMENT FOR FINANCIAL EDUCATION

LEARNING TO GIVE

Instructions Your Money Your Community Nonprofit Family Giving Resources

Managing Your Money

Money management is a skill that you will use for the rest of your life. It's worth learning to manage your money wisely now. This way, you'll get off to a good start in the world of finances.

In this section, you'll learn the main principles of money management. Money issues may seem complex. But the principles of managing money are actually simple. It's putting them into practice that takes discipline.

To manage your money well, you'll need a good budget or spending plan. To determine your budget, you must first know your income. You must also make a commitment to saving. Finally, you'll plan your expenses. As part of your planning, you may set aside money to start investing. You can also donate to support your community.

In this section:

> Key to success
> Income
> Saving
> Spending
> Investing
> Donating
> Spending plan
> Resources

Some money management Web sites, such as this one for www. moneysmartchoices.org, offer free tools to help teens plan and set up a budget.

spreadsheet program. If you don't have a computer, then make your budget in a notebook that is dedicated for that purpose. First, enter a title such as "Monthly Budget" and a date. Next, make two sections. Label the top section "Net Income." Label the bottom section "Expenses." Make five columns in each section. You are ready to begin entering information into your monthly budget.

Figuring Income

Making a budget begins with your income. You already know what your average net income is for one week. Now,

Budgeting Tools and Information Protection on the Internet

Some Web sites provide free budgeting tools. They might have chat rooms where you can share ideas about money with others. But be careful about sharing personal and financial information online. Do not give anyone your passwords or personal identification numbers (PINs). Protect your identity and money from Internet ID theft. Look for and read the privacy statements on Web sites. Privacy statements might be on Web sites' homepages or in the "About" or "FAQ" section. Look for secure Web pages. Signals that you have found one include a screen notice that you are in a secure Web site or a closed key in the bottom corner of the Web page. Another sign is "https" (hypertext transfer protocols) as the first letters of the Internet address you are viewing, which means that you are using a site that transfers data securely over the Internet.

determine your average net income for one month. In the "Net Income" section of your budget, enter your average sources of regular (ongoing) income and the amount for each income source for one month. Include your allowance and earnings from all jobs. If you are paid weekly, then multiply your net pay from your paycheck by 52, divide by 12, and enter that amount. If you are paid biweekly (every two weeks), then multiply your net pay by 26, divide by 12, and enter that amount.

Include other regular income, such as interest on savings accounts. You might get income from a savings account quarterly (every three months). To figure out this amount as monthly income, divide the interest by three. For example, if you get $30 every quarter as interest income, then divide $30 by three. You receive $10 every month as interest income.

Your income might vary from month to month. You might work more hours during the summer because you are not in school. As a result, your income in the summer might be higher than in the winter. Use the lowest monthly income for your budget.

Do not include any uncertain sources of money as income. You cannot depend on unexpected income. Money gifts, cash from selling things, money from odd jobs, or birthday and holiday gifts are not regular income sources.

Finish entering all regular sources of income for a month. Then, add all your income amounts. Enter this amount in "Total Monthly Income."

Figuring Expenses

The next part of a budget is your expenses and how much money you plan to spend on each expense. You already know your expenses for one week. To make your budget, look more closely at your monthly expenses.

Look over your weekly spending expenses from chapter 1. Think about your spending habits and financial goals. What are your spending priorities? What do you absolutely need? What are you saving for? How much do you plan to save short term and long term? How much do you need for future expenses, such as a new computer or college? Do you have an emergency fund? Do you share your money with causes that are important to you?

Some teens use cash to pay for goods and services. Using cash helps them stay within their budget.

Review past bills and saved receipts to help you estimate some expenses. Also, look at records, cancelled checks, and credit card and bank statements. To plan for inflation, set your expense budget a little higher. Inflation is an increase in the price of goods or services that you buy. It makes things more expensive.

Fixed Expenses

You must pay fixed expenses regularly. Fixed expenses might include car payments, auto insurance, and rent for an apartment.

Monthly Budget

		Budget	Actual
Net Income	Average pay from job	$640	$649
	Interest income	$ 5	$ 5
	Other	$ 0	$ 0
Total Monthly Income		$645	$654
Expenses			
Fixed Expenses	Car payment	$150	$146
	Car insurance	$205	$205
	Cell phone	$ 15	$ 28
	Parking and tolls	$ 12	$ 18
	Other	$ 0	$ 0
Variable Expenses			
Savings	Emergency fund	$ 20	$ 20
	Savings/investments	$ 18	$ 10
	Short-term savings (jacket)	$ 10	$ 5
	Medium-term savings (travel)	$ 20	$ 0
	Long-term savings (college)	$ 20	$ 30
Ongoing Variable Expenses	Clothing and shoes	$ 60	$ 85
	School expenses	$ 15	$ 18
	Entertainment and gifts	$ 40	$ 48
	Transportation/gas	$ 40	$ 56
	Personal items	$ 15	$ 26
Sharing	Local animal shelter	$ 5	$ 0
Total Expenses/Savings/Sharing		$645	$695
Income Minus Expenses		$ 0	-$ 41

Other fixed expenses might be cell phone bills, parking fees, public transportation fares, and dues.

You might have payments that are due once a year, such as a car license fee. To figure out an annual fee for your monthly budget, divide the annual fee by 12. Enter that amount in your budget. For example, divide an annual auto license fee of $192 by 12 to get a monthly amount of $16.

If you pay your auto insurance twice each year, then add the two payments to get the total. Divide the total by 12 to get the monthly amount. What is the monthly amount of two auto insurance payments of $616 and $627?

$616 + $627 = $1,243 (total amount)
$1,243 ÷ 12 = $104 (monthly amount)

Remember to round up to the nearest dollar.

Variable Expenses

After paying for fixed expenses, you probably have money left over. You can use this disposable income to pay for variable, or non-fixed, expenses. Variable expenses typically change over time. Your variable expenses might include food, clothes and shoes, household and personal items, transportation and car upkeep, school expenses, entertainment and gifts, magazine subscriptions, and other categories. What you actually spend on variable expenses might be different from what you have budgeted for. Be sure to include variable expenses in your budget. You might want to estimate your variable expenses. To arrive at realistic estimates, review your receipts, bills, online transactions, and other records from the past two or three months.

Variable expenses include savings and sharing. Saving is putting money away for emergencies and short-term,

By having a firm grasp of your fixed expenses, you will know how much you can spend on variable expenses, such as personal items.

medium-term, and long-term goals. A good budget includes an emergency fund. Each month, set money aside to prepare for unexpected events like car repairs. You might want to set aside 5 percent of your monthly income for emergencies. For example, if your monthly income is $824, then multiply that amount by 5 percent: $824 × .05 = $41. Include $41 every month in your budget for emergencies.

Decide how much to set aside for your other savings goals. What financial goals are important to you now and in the future? When do you want to reach these goals? Include the amounts for savings in your budget. Saving regularly can help you reach goals such as buying a car or going on a vacation. To help you save, keep your bank accounts and any investment information up to date.

Sharing, or giving to causes, is another variable expense. Decide what causes are important to you. Then, decide how much money you want to set aside each month for sharing. Include that amount in your budget.

Once you have your total income and total expenses, balance your budget for the month. To balance your budget, subtract your expenses from your income. Do you have enough income to pay for your expenses? Do you have money left over? If it's a negative number, then you are spending more money than you have.

Trying Out Your Budget

If your income did not equal your expenses, then you are in need of a balanced budget. Check your expenses and income. Perhaps you did not include all your expenses, or you were unrealistic about your expenses. Maybe you did not include some monthly income, or you included an uncertain source of income.

Some teens use spreadsheets to set up and maintain a budget. Paper and pencil work, too. Determine what works best for you and then stick with your method.

If your total income and total expenses for the month are equal, then you have a balanced budget. A balanced budget is your goal. Usually, a balanced budget takes some time and practice to achieve.

You might want to make some changes to your monthly budget at this point. Or, you might want to follow your budget for a month. At the end of the month, record your actual income and expenses. Find the difference between your budgeted income and expenses. Do you need to adjust your budget now? Your budget is a work in progress. Evaluating and adjusting your budget are important steps in managing your money.

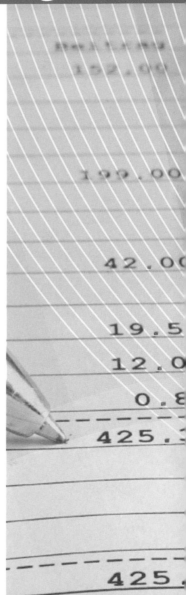

Chapter 3
Evaluating and Adjusting Your Budget

When you have money, you need to decide whether to spend or save it. How much you spend and save is up to you. Practicing good money management takes some time and thought. By planning ahead with your budget, you can avoid mistakes that will cost you money.

When you first set up your budget, you might forget to include some expenses and categories. You might be spending more on wants than needs (luxuries vs. necessities). If you have not planned and budgeted for your financial goals, then you might not be saving enough money. As a result, you might not reach your financial goals.

Needs and Wants

Needs are things you must have, such as clothing and shoes. Wants are things you would like to have. A designer T-shirt or designer shoes are wants. You probably have ideas about needs and wants that are different from those of your friends. Transportation for work is a need. To get to and from work, you might use the city bus, subway, or train. You would view a car for going

To create a money goal, you need to determine the cost of the product or service. These teens are checking out which laptop to buy and the cost.

to work as a want. Your friend, however, might live in the country and not have access to city transportation. Your friend would view a car for going to work as a need.

To make a realistic budget, decide what is important to you. Determine what things you could not live without and put them in your budget. Then, determine the wants that are most important to you and include them.

Know Your Spending and Saving Patterns

Budgeting involves making spending and saving choices. How do you spend your money? How much money do you really need? What are you willing to give up to buy or save for what you want? Do you regularly save some money? Is investing money important to you?

To make a realistic budget, you need to know your spending and saving patterns. Your fixed expenses are known once you decide what you cannot live without. Subtract these needs from your income. The money remaining is what you can spend on your wants.

Perhaps you have not budgeted enough for savings. Look at your variable expenses. Are you downloading songs to your MP3 player every week? Downloading music is probably a want, not a need. Could you live happily if you download fewer songs every other week or even once a

You can use your budget to help you plan to buy something that you really want, such as a new video game.

month? This change provides more savings for your needs or financial goals.

If your needs are greater than your income, then consider increasing your income. One option is to work odd jobs to supplement your income. You might decide to babysit two Fridays every month. You would gain two financial benefits: extra income and not spending money on those Friday evenings.

Grow good money habits. Save first when you get paid. Put your money into savings to reach your financial goals. If you have money for wants, then budget for occasional impulse buying. To help you manage your money, make a list of what you need before you shop. Stick to your list when shopping.

Setting Financial Goals

The most important part of managing your money is determining what is important to you. First, determine your short-term (1 month–12 months), medium-term (13 months–24 months), and long-term (25 months–60 months) financial goals. Set goals based on your values, not on what your friends or others have or want. Make your goals specific and measurable: "Save $25 a week for 20 weeks until I have enough money to buy a computer." Put your financial goals in writing to make them more concrete. Next, prioritize your goals. Then, choose the goals you want to work toward.

Say a short-term goal is to buy a $1,000 computer in five months. If you budget $25 a week, then you will not make your goal: $25 × 20 weeks = $500. Instead, you decide to save $50 for 20 weeks. Then, you will reach your goal: $50 × 20 weeks = $1,000. Or, you might decide to wait longer and save $25 a week for 10 months: $25 × 40 weeks = $1,000.

Sometimes, figuring out how much a product or service will cost can be difficult. A parent or guardian can help you determine realistic costs of your financial goals.

A medium-term goal might be to put 10 percent of your income into savings for college. Look over your budget. Perhaps you can reach this goal by cutting your entertainment expenses by 10 percent.

To reach your financial goals, you need to save money. You might also want to support your community or organizations that are important to you. Think about support that you can offer to organizations like the American Red Cross, American Heart Association, Humane Society of the United States, or an environmental organization. Perhaps you might want to offer support to your public library, a local animal shelter, or a local community center.

Evaluating and Adjusting Your Budget

Evaluating and adjusting your budget are important steps. Review your budget after one month to see if it is helping you reach your financial goals. You might need to adjust categories.

Continue evaluating your budget monthly, even if it is balancing. Your financial goals, needs, and wants will change over time. Your income will probably change. Your expenses might also change because of increases in taxes and inflation. Keeping your budget up to date is vital to having your budget work for you.

Making Your Budget Work

A successful budget is very useful, but it can take time to create. Budgeting might be a new habit for you. It takes time and practice to learn something new. Here are some things to keep in mind when making a budget:

Include an emergency fund in your budget to prepare for unexpected events. Perhaps your car won't start. After it is towed to an auto repair shop, you learn that your car needs a new alternator. You might use your entire emergency fund to pay for the tow and repairs. Reset your financial goals and adjust your budget to build your emergency fund.

You may have randomly decided which categories to cut down when making your budget. At first, you might not know if the amounts will work. As you work with and evaluate your budget, you may need to increase the amounts in certain categories, such as savings or gas. Decrease the amounts in nonessential categories. For example, cut eating at fast-food restaurants for one month. Save that money to buy a new printer or add to your emergency fund.

Have you set realistic financial goals? Perhaps you are saving to buy a car. According to your budget, it will take 18 months to reach this goal. Sticking with your budget for so long might be difficult. To help you reach your goals, set small milestones along the way. Reward yourself at each milestone. You might buy a DVD if you do not eat at fast-food restaurants

You may need to use your emergency funds for towing and unexpected car repairs.

for a month. Little rewards can help you stick to your budget.

Do you have some money for fun in your budget? Slashing your entertainment dollars too much might set you up to fail. You might overspend if you feel deprived. If your budget is tight, though, you might have to limit your fun money to $20 or less per month.

Write down your financial goals. Put them next to your cash, credit, or debit card in your wallet or purse. Look over your goals before you buy something to help you stick to your budget. You might avoid stores in which you overspend.

Adjusting and evaluating your budget takes some time. Are you taking enough time? Aim to work on your budget once a month or try shorter blocks of time. Work five minutes each day, or 30 minutes every week. Once you reach a large financial goal, set a new goal or goals and adjust your budget. Over time, your needs will change, and so will your budget. Remember to include savings in your expenses because it is money put away for future expenses.

CHAPTER 4

Budgeting and Saving

Budgeting helps you save money and develop a balance between saving and spending. By having a "Savings" category in your budget, you will put money into savings each month. You move toward your financial goals as you save money.

Why Save?

Saving helps you care for yourself both short term and long term. You might have expenses you did not expect. Or, you might want money to buy something special. If you have budgeted for savings, then you will have that money when you need it.

Start a savings plan. Look again at your short-term, medium-term, and long-term financial goals from chapter 3. When you budget for your goals, put "Savings" as your first expense. Make saving a habit by always paying yourself first. How much should you save? A good rule is to save 10 percent of your income. You might be able to save more depending on your financial goals.

Many teens save a regular amount from each paycheck or an allowance and deposit it into a savings account.

Setting up an emergency fund is an important short-term savings goal. Use emergency funds to pay for unexpected repairs on your car, for example. You probably also have some fun short-term goals, such as buying sports gear or a bike.

Medium-term and long-term financial goals are future goals. Future goals might include saving money for college, a vacation, or a different car. Future financial goals generally require more money than short-term goals. To meet future goals, you typically save small amounts of money over a long period of time.

Savings Products

Are you saving money by hiding it in an old sock? A better idea is to start a savings account at a bank. By putting your money away, you won't be as tempted to spend it. You can also watch your savings grow because banks pay you interest for keeping your money. Interest is paid as a percentage of the amount that you deposit. You can set up one savings account. Or, you might want to set up three savings accounts to separate long-term, medium-term, and short-term savings goals.

Savings products offered by banks are safe places to put your money. The federal government through the Federal Deposit Insurance Corporation (FDIC) insures bank deposits up to $100,000 per bank. In 2008, the FDIC temporarily increased the protected amount to $250,000 through December 2009. Your savings are available to you when you need them. Savings products offered by banks include savings accounts, money market accounts, certificates of deposit (CDs), and U.S. savings bonds.

Money market accounts require a large deposit and a large minimum balance. Money market accounts earn more interest than a regular savings account. CDs require that you deposit money for a specific amount of time, such as six months or a year. CDs earn more interest than money market and savings accounts. You pay a large fee if you take out your money early from a CD.

When you buy a U.S. savings bond, you pay half its face value. A $100 savings bond would cost you $50. When the bond matures in 20 years, you can cash it for its face value of $100. Some savings bonds earn interest after they mature.

The Power of Compounding

The key to saving is to make your money work for you through compounding. With compounding, you earn interest on the money that you save and on the interest the money earns. The power of compounding comes with time. The sooner you start saving, the more your money can work for you.

Say that you buy a can of soda for $1 every day for a year. That adds up to $365. Instead, put that $365 into a savings account earning 5 percent per year. You would have $383 at the end of one year. In five years, your total would be $483. At the end of 30 years, your total would be $1,564. Even a small amount of savings can add up to big money because of compounding over time.

Investing

You can make your money grow by investing in stocks, bonds, mutual funds, or other money tools. Unlike bank savings, the federal government does not insure invested money. You have a higher risk of losing your money by investing than by savings. So, why might you want to invest? You have the opportunity to earn more money with investments than with savings.

You might invest by buying stocks of a company. If the value of the stock goes up, then the company pays you money when you sell the stock. A company might also pay you dividends, which are the part of a company's profit paid to its stockholders. Stock value depends on how well the company is doing, how much people will pay for the stock, and the world economy. If the company does poorly, then you might lose some or all of your investment.

Experts at financial institutions can help you or your investment club learn about investing.

Another investment is bonds. A public company or a local, state, or national government might sell bonds to raise money. When you buy bonds, an organization pays you interest on your money. It also promises to return your money on a set due date, perhaps in 10 years. Bonds generally are less risky than stocks.

Mutual funds are another option for investing. A mutual fund is a pool of money run by trained professionals. The professionals invest in a mix of stocks, bonds, and other items. Every mutual fund has a different level of risk and opportunities to earn money.

You might decide to join an investment club, which is often offered in schools. In these clubs, a group of people makes decisions on investing. They pool their money to make investments. The group votes to buy or sell stocks, bonds, mutual funds, or other items.

Paper and Plastic Money

Many teens keep their money in both a checking account and a savings account. You write a check to pay for something with money in your checking account. You can write paper checks or use online checks. Checks are safer to carry and send than cash.

Do you pay for goods and services with paper money, plastic money, or both? Paying by credit or debit card can work well, as long as you stay within your budgeted expenses.

An automatic teller machine (ATM) card typically comes with your bank account. Using an ATM card and machine, you can make deposits to or get money from your bank accounts. Some banks charge a fee for every use of an ATM or for not using an ATM associated with your bank.

Using debit cards or credit cards are other ways to pay for goods and services. When you use a debit card, you pay now. A store takes money from your checking or savings account immediately to pay for something. Some debit cards have monthly fees. Others charge a fee for each use. Banks charge overdraft fees if you use your debit card without having enough money deposited in your account.

Unlike with debit cards, you pay later with credit cards. A credit card lets you borrow money. When you use a credit card, a store gets the money you owe from a bank. After about a month, the bank totals your credit card charges and sends you a bill. You can pay the whole bill, or you can pay some of what you owe and pay the rest later. The bank charges interest on the amount you do not pay back.

Some people continue to put new charges on their credit card and never pay the entire amount. Over time, they could owe a lot of money to their bank. This debt could affect their credit score, a number that shows the credit risk of a person. A person with a low credit score might have difficulty getting a loan from a bank for school costs or to buy a car.

Sometimes, you might find that saving is difficult. You might be tempted to withdraw your savings to buy something you want now instead of saving toward a future goal. Keep your financial goals in mind. Stick to your savings plan. Wise spending can help you keep more of your money for savings.

Ten Great Questions to Ask
a Professional Financial Adviser

1 How much time does it take to set up a budget?

2 How much money should I keep in an emergency fund?

3 Should I save my money in a savings account, a money market account, a CD, savings bonds, or some combination of these?

4 When should I use a debit card or a credit card?

5 How many credit cards should I have?

6 How do I establish a good credit score?

7 Should I take out a loan or pay cash to buy a car?

8 What are the best types of investments for me: stocks, bonds, or mutual funds?

9 Are collectibles, such as gold or silver coins, a good investment?

10 Should I ask a third party to review my budget once a year?

CHAPTER 5

Budgeting and Spending

Expenses in your budget include both savings and spending. After setting aside money in your budget for savings, you have income left for other expenses. Your spending should cover both your needs and your wants. You can set spending priorities by determining your needs from your wants.

Think Before Spending

After following your budget for a month or longer, do you usually spend more than your income? You have two choices to deal with this. One option is to increase your income. However, you might not be able to work more hours. Besides work, you need time for school and studies, family, recreation, and other activities that are important to you.

A second option is to reduce your spending. Practice discipline and control in your spending habits. For costly items, make buying decisions based on careful thought and research. Avoid impulse buying. Keep your receipts so that you can return unnecessary items.

Impulsive purchases made on the Internet can quickly ruin your budget if you do not pay attention to your needs versus your wants.

Try to be thoughtful about spending. Learn to do this by removing your emotions from your money. Say you are out with friends and see a tempting pair of shoes in a store. Before buying, ask yourself if these shoes are a necessity or a want. If you made a list of necessities, would the shoes be on your list? Would your life change for the better if you owned these shoes? If the answer is no, then do not buy them.

You might find it difficult to pass on the latest cell phone if all of your friends have it. Think about your personal values. Ignore advertisers and the values of your peers. Although peers can influence you, remember that you make your own spending decisions.

Be realistic about your spending strengths and weaknesses. Can you go to a mall without buying something? Do you always buy something at your favorite store? Avoid these places until you can limit your spending. You might want to sleep on a large buying decision. Another method is to write what you want to buy on a piece of paper. Put the paper away for a week or longer. Time might blunt your desire to buy the item.

Spend Wisely

To gain more expense money, look at your habits. If you buy soda or coffee, consider drinking water from the fountains at school for free. Bring your own water, juice, or snacks in reusable containers from home. Limit sodas and coffees.

Plan ahead when you drive, and group small trips together to use gas efficiently. Keep your car tuned up and tires inflated for better gas mileage. Perhaps using a carpool or taking public transportation will save you money.

Showing your student ID might get you savings on movies, transportation, and meals. Many programs have discounts for students. If you are not sure, ask about student discounts.

As a student, you may be able to find discounts and sales. A savvy shopper stays alert for ways to save money.

Shop at used clothing and thrift stores for clothes, accessories, furniture, and other items. Before you buy, ask yourself: What will you do with the item? Where will you store it? What are the cleaning costs? Are repairs costly?

Comparison shopping helps you stay within your budget and live within your means. As a comparison shopper, you want to buy high-quality items at the lowest price. As you research items, ask yourself: Do you need a brand name? If yes, then what brand? Where might you buy the item? Do you need to buy now or later? Can the items be new or used? Do you need to earn more money to buy any items? Use comparison shopping Web sites to evaluate prices.

Comparison Shopping for Cars

Use comparison shopping to help you decide on the type of car that you can afford. First, list the costs of owning a car. Your list might include car payments, gas, insurance, repairs, and license. Next, check the values and repair history of cars that you want to buy. Read car reviews and car ratings. Then, ask an insurance agent for insurance costs on cars that you might want. The type of car influences the cost of insurance.

Watch Out for Fees

Do you need to adjust your spending to avoid bank fees? Banks often charge fees on everything from using their online bill-paying service to a negative account balance. You might be charged a fee if your balance is negative for even a few minutes. Some banks charge a monthly fee for checking accounts. Others do not charge a monthly fee if you maintain a specified minimum balance. Banks charge a stop-payment fee to stop a check or an automatic bill payment.

ATM fees can quickly add up. Banks might charge a fee every time you use an ATM. If you use an ATM that belongs to another bank, your bank and the company that owns the ATM will both charge you fees.

If you spend more than you have in your account, your balance will be negative. Your bank will charge non-sufficient fees (NSF) for every check or debit that you transact. The company will also charge you a fee. You will still owe the company the amount on the check or in the debit transaction.

Bargain Shopping

Everyone likes to get a bargain or the best value on something. To determine what items are bargains, compare both price and quality. If you compare a single item at different stores, the item with the lower price is likely the better buy. Do a little math to find the better price on multiple items in a package.

For example, which is the better bargain: a two-pack of socks for $4.99, or a four-pack of socks for $7.99? Divide the cost by the amount to find the price per unit (pairs of socks):

$4.99 ÷ 2 = $2.50 per unit
$7.99 ÷ 4 = $2.00 per unit

The four-pack of socks is a better bargain.

Along with price, compare quality to determine the value. Which pair of socks is the better value: the thick two-pack, or the thin four-pack? Thick socks last longer than thin socks. The two-pack socks are the better value.

Stores often put items on sale to entice people to buy them. If a pair of $30 jeans are discounted 20 percent, then how much are they? To find the answer, change 20 percent to a decimal, multiply the price by the discount, and subtract the discount from the price:

20% = .20
$30 × .20 = $6
$30 − $6 = $24

The jeans cost $24.

Sometimes, stores further discount items. You might see a sign that reads "Take an additional 15 percent off" on $30 jeans that have already been discounted 20 percent. How much are the jeans? The discount is not the sum of the two percents added together (20% + 15% = 35%). To find the discounted price, figure each discount separately:

$30 × .20 = $6
$30 − $6 = $24 (price of jeans discounted 20 percent)

$24 × .15 = $3.60
$24 − $3.60 = $20.40 (price of jeans discounted 20 percent, plus another 15 percent discount)

The jeans cost $20.40.

Be aware of bait-and-switch methods. For instance, a store might entice you with great bargains. Once you are in the store, you are told the items are not available. Only similar and more costly items are for sale. This is deceptive advertising. Some car dealers use the bait-and-switch method. They might advertise a new car for $10,000 (bait). When you get to the car lot, however, the salespeople say that all of those cars are gone. Instead, they have similar cars that cost more (switch).

Consumer Rights and Responsibilities

As a consumer of goods and services, you have certain rights and responsibilities. Four basic consumer rights are the right to safety, the right to be informed, the right to choose, and the right to be heard. Different agencies and organizations protect and help consumers with complaints. These include consumer

One way to check for product safety issues is by reading government notices, such as those posted on the U.S. Consumer Product Safety Commission's site (www.cpsc.gov), on the Internet.

affairs bureaus, media action programs, private consumer groups, licensing boards, and government services.

Government agencies include the Consumer Product Safety Commission (CPSC), which protects consumers against harmful products. The CPSC can ban or recall dangerous products. The Federal Trade Commission (FTC) prevents the unfair, false, or deceptive advertising of goods and services. The Federal Citizen Information Center (FCIC) provides consumer information by providing the free *Consumer Information Catalog* four times a year. The Food and Drug Administration (FDA) ensures that manufacturers' medicines are labeled, safe, and effective for their intended use.

Some companies are reputable, and some are not. Federal and state agencies cannot check all companies that sell in malls, in catalogs, on television, over the telephone, and on the Web. As a consumer, you are responsible for researching the safety of products. Report any consumer fraud. You have a responsibility to complain when necessary and to make sure your complaints are dealt with fairly.

If you are a catalog shopper, consider all costs for purchases, including shipping and taxes. In addition, some companies charge a restocking fee for returns.

Keep Up Your Budget

Sometimes, budgets can fail. If your budget is not working, look it over to see if you have unrealistic expenses. Have you forgotten some items or expenses? Do you have a written budget? Are you spending enough time working with your budget? Perhaps you have forgotten to budget money to do some fun things.

A good budget is geared toward your goals and is based on your needs and wants. You can change your budget if it is not working or if you have large changes in your life, such as getting a car. Your budget is an important tool for your financial well-being now and in the future.

Glossary

bond A promise to pay a certain amount on a certain date, issued by a company or government, to borrow money.

budget A plan for how to spend and save your money.

certificate of deposit (CD) A type of savings in which money is deposited for a certain period of time to earn a specific rate of interest.

checking account A bank account that allows the person to take out money, pay bills, or buy things by writing checks.

comparison shopping Researching brands to buy the highest quality at the lowest price.

compound interest The interest earned on both the original amount and any previous interest added to the balance.

credit An agreement in which someone buys something now and promises to pay for it later.

credit score A number that indicates a person's credit risk.

deductions Amounts withheld, or taken out of gross pay, such as federal and income taxes, Social Security tax, and Medicare tax.

dividend Portion of a company's profits paid to stockholders.

earnings Money received for doing work.

expenses Goods and services that people pay for with their money.

fixed expenses Expenses that stay the same and must be paid from month to month, such as rent.

gross pay The total amount earned before deductions are subtracted.

income Money earned for doing work, or received from savings, investments, or gifts.

interest Money that banks pay for using money deposited in accounts.

investing The risking of money and time to get more money in return.

loan A sum of money borrowed for a certain amount of time.

mutual fund An investment run by professionals in which people pool their money to buy stocks, bonds, and other items.

overdraft fee A payment for having a negative balance in an account.

savings account A bank account in which money is deposited for safekeeping.

savings bonds Bonds issued by the federal government sold at half their face value.

stock An investment in the ownership of a company.

transaction Any business, such as a deposit or withdrawal, done with a bank.

variable expenses Expenses that vary from month to month.

For More Information

Canadian Bankers Association
Box 348
Commerce Court West
199 Bay Street, 30th Floor
Toronto, ON M5L 1G2
Canada
(800) 263-0231
Web site: http://www.cba.ca
The Canadian Bankers Association provides information for
teens to learn about money, budgeting, credit, invest-
ments, goal setting, and banking in Canada.

Certified Financial Planner Board of Standards
1670 Broadway, Suite 600
Denver, CO 80202
(888) 237-6275
Web site: http://www.cfp.net/learn
This organization offers personal financial planning information. You can find local certified financial planners on
its Web site.

Consumer Federation of America
1620 I Street NW, Suite 200
Washington, DC 20006
(202) 387-6121
Web site: http://www.consumerfed.org
Consumer Federation of America is an advocacy, research,
and education organization providing information and
resources on personal finances, including money management and budgeting.

Federal Deposit Insurance Corporation (FDIC)
550 Seventeenth Street NW
Washington, DC 20429
(877) 275-3342
Web site: http://www.fdic.gov
An independent agency of the U.S. government, the FDIC
protects individuals against the loss of deposits. This
agency also provides information on deposit insurance,
shopping for financial services, understanding consumer
rights, and avoiding financial fraud.

Financial Literacy and Education Commission
U.S. Department of the Treasury
1500 Pennsylvania Avenue NW
Washington, DC 20220
(888) MY-MONEY (696-6639)
Web site: http://www.mymoney.gov
The Financial Literacy and Education Commission offers a variety
of information on money management and budgeting.

Financial Planners Standards Council
902–375 University Avenue
Toronto, ON M5G 2J5
Canada
(800) 305-9886
Web site: http://www.fpsccanada.org
The Financial Planners Standards Council provides information
and resources for teens on personal finance, budgeting,
savings, investments, and more.

Jump$tart
919 Eighteenth Street NW, Suite 300
Washington, DC 20006

(888) 45-EDUCATE (453-3822)
Web site: http://www.jumpstartcoalition.org
Jump$tart offers information on money management,
budgeting, goal setting, credit, and investing. Go to its
clearinghouse to find a list of books and other print
materials, CDs, DVDs, videos, and Web sites.

National Council on Economic Education
1140 Avenue of the Americas
New York, NY 10036
(800) 338-1192
Web site: http://www.ncee.net
This organization provides a personal finance Web site for
teens at www.italladdsup.org, which covers budgeting,
goal setting, credit, saving, and investing.

National Endowment for Financial Education
5299 DTC Boulevard, Suite 1300
Greenwood Village, CO 80111
(303) 741-6333
Web site: http://www.nefe.org
This organization offers information and resources on
money management, budgeting, setting financial goals,
and more.

Web Sites

Due to the changing nature of Internet links, Rosen Publishing
has developed an online list of Web sites related to the subject
of this book. This site is updated regularly. Please use this link
to access the list:

http://www.rosenlinks.com/gsm/budg

For Further Reading

Brancato, Robin. *Money: The Ultimate Teen Guide*. Blue Ridge Summit, PA: The Scarecrow Press, 2006.

Cauvier, Denis, and Alan Lysaght. *The ABCs of Making Money 4 Teens.* Ogdensburg, NY: Wealth Solutions Press, 2005.

Collins, Robyn, and Kimberly Spinks Burleson. *Prepare to Be a Teen Millionaire*. Deerfield Beach, FL: HCI, 2008.

Denega, Danielle. *Smart Money: How to Manage Your Cash*. London, England: Franklin Watts, 2008.

Foster, Chad. *Financial Literacy for Teens*. Conyers, GA: Rising Books, 2004.

Holmberg, Joshua, and David Bruzzese. *The Teen's Guide to Personal Finance: Basic Concepts in Personal Finance That Every Teen Should Know*. Littleton, CO: iUniverse, 2008.

Morris, Virginia B., and Kenneth M. Morris. *A Woman's Guide to Investing*. New York, NY: Lightbulb Press, 2005.

Richards, Kristi. *Making, Managing, and Milking Your Money: What Every Teen Needs to Know*. Charleston, SC: BookSurge Publishing, 2003.

Silver, Don. *High School Money Book*. Los Angeles, CA: Adams-Hall Publishing, 2007.

Stahl, Mike. *Early to Rise: A Young Adult's Guide to Investing and Financial Decisions That Can Shape Your Life*. Los Angeles, CA: Silver Lake Publishing, 2005.

Bibliography

American Institute of Certified Public Accountants. "Teaching Your Teen About Money." 2007. Retrieved July 2, 2008 (http://www.360financialliteracy.org/Life+Stages/Childhood/Articles/Teaching+your+teen+about+money.htm).

Bodnar, Janet. *Raising Money Smart Kids: What They Need to Know About Money and How to Tell Them.* New York, NY: Kaplan Business, 2005.

Charles Schwab. "Teens & Money 2007 Survey Findings: Insights into Money Attitudes, Behaviors, and Concerns of Teens." 2007. Retrieved July 2, 2008 (http://www.aboutschwab.com/teensurvey2007.pdf).

CUSucceed.net. "CU Succeed: Teens Financial Network." 2008. Retrieved July 9, 2008 (http://www.cusucceed.net/resources.php).

FDIC.gov. "Start Smart: Money Management for Teens." *FDIC Consumer News*, Summer 2006. Retrieved July 6, 2008 (http://www.fdic.gov/CONSUMERS/CONSUMER/news/cnsum06/index.html).

Federal Deposit Insurance Corporation. "How to Ace Your First Test Managing Real Money in the Real World." *FDIC Consumer News*, Spring 2008, pp. 5–6.

Federal Deposit Insurance Corporation. "What to Know Before Declaring Your Financial Independence." *FDIC Consumer News*, Spring 2008, pp. 6–7.

Garber, Dustin. "What's the Deal with Debit?" CUSucceed.net, 2008. Retrieved July 21, 2008 (http://www.cusucceed.net/article.php?arttable=teenArticles&recnum=27#top).

Godfrey, Neale S., and Carolina Edwards. *Money Doesn't Grow on Trees: A Parent's Guide to Raising Financially Responsible Children.* New York, NY: Fireside, 2006.

GSA Office of Citizen Services and Communications. *Consumer Action Handbook*. Washington, DC: Federal Citizen Information Center, 2008.

Jones, K. C. "Consumers Spend Less, Comparison Shop Online." *Information Week*, July 30, 2008. Retrieved July 31, 2008 (http://www.informationweek.com/news/internet/retail/showArticle.jhtml?articleID=209900621).

Learning to Give and National Endowment for Financial Education. "Managing Your Money." 2008. Retrieved July 7, 2008 (http://www.moneysmartchoices.org/your_money/your_money.html).

MetLife Consumer Education Center and American Association of Individual Investors. *Building Financial Freedom*. New York, NY: MetLife, 2006.

Missouri Economic Research and Information Center. "Teaching Your Teen About Money." 2005. Retrieved July 8, 2008 (http://ded.mo.gov/researchandplanning/pdfs/teenmoney.pdf).

Money Instructor. "Sample Monthly Household Budget." 2005. Retrieved July 9, 2008 (http://www.moneyinstructor.com/art/budgetsample.asp).

Office of Investor Education and Advocacy. *Get the Facts on Savings and Investing*. Washington, DC: U.S. Securities and Exchange Commission, 2007.

Orman, Suze. *The Money Book for the Young, Fabulous & Broke*. New York, NY: Riverhead Trade, 2007.

PracticalMoneySkills.com. "Setting Up a Personal Budget." 2008. Retrieved July 9, 2008 (http://www.practicalmoneyskills.com/english/pdf/teachers/lev_3/lesson_03/3_4.pdf).

Rhode Island Department of Health. "Teaching Your Teen About Money." 2008. Retrieved July 7, 2008 (http://www.health.ri.gov/family/ofyss/teens/tips/Tip38.php).

University of California Cooperative Extension. "Money Talks Teen Guides." 2007. Retrieved July 6, 2008 (http://www.moneytalks.ucr.edu/english/newsletters/newsletters_home.html).

USA Weekend. "Teaching Teens About Money Management." 1999. Retrieved July 7, 2008 (http://www.usaweekend.com/classroom/PDF_guides/guide_money99.pdf).

Wells Fargo. "Hands on Banking: Young Adults Teacher's Guide." 2005. Retrieved July 6, 2008 (http://www.handsonbanking.org/nav_elements/teachers_guide_PDF/YA_T_Guide.pdf).

Index

A

allowance, 6, 7, 10, 11, 19
ATM cards, 41

B

bank fees, 41, 47–48
bargain shopping, 48–49
budget/budgeting
    balancing, 14–16, 26, 32
    evaluating and adjusting,
        27–34
    lack of skill in, 11
    making it work, 32–34, 52
    myths and facts about, 15
    purpose of, 4–6, 7, 15, 16,
        17, 27
    setting up monthly, 17–26
    using Web sites for, 19

C

certificates of deposit (CDs), 37
checking accounts, 40–41, 47
comparison shopping, 46, 47
compounding, 38
consumer rights and responsibilities,
        49–51
credit cards, 41

D

debit cards, 41
debt, having, 10, 11

E

emergency fund, 20, 23, 25,
        32, 33, 36
expenses, 6, 7
    figuring, 20–25
    fixed, 17, 21–23, 29
    monthly record of, 16
    as part of budget, 6, 8,
        20–25, 43
    subtracting from income,
        14–16, 25
    variable, 17, 23–25, 29–30
    weekly record of, 12–16,
        17, 20

F

financial adviser, questions to
        ask a, 42

G

goals, financial/money, 7, 15, 17,
        20, 25, 27, 30, 32, 34,
        35–36, 37
    setting, 30–31, 33
gross pay, 8

I

income, 6, 7, 43
    figuring, 18–20
    as part of budget, 6, 8, 10–11,
        18–20

About the Author

Judy Monroe Peterson holds two master's degrees and is the author of numerous educational books for young people. She is a former technical, health care, and academic librarian and college faculty member; a research scientist; and a curriculum editor with more than 25 years of experience. She has taught courses at 3M, the University of Minnesota, and Lake Superior College. Currently, she is a writer and editor of K–12 and post–high school curriculum materials on a variety of subjects, including life skills.

Photo Credits

Cover (foreground) © www.istockphoto.com/Justin Horrocks; cover, p. 1 (top) © www.istockphoto.com/Milan Klusacek; cover, p. 1 (middle) © www.istockphoto.com/David Lewis; cover, p. 1 (bottom) © www.istockphoto.com/Damir Cudic; pp. 4–5, 26 Shutterstock.com; pp. 8, 17, 27, 35, 43 © www.istockphoto.com/dwphotos; p. 9 © Francisco Cruz/SuperStock; p. 14 © Spencer Grant/PhotoEdit; p. 21 © David Young-Wolff/PhotoEdit; p. 24 © www.istockphoto.com/Gloria-Leigh Logan; p. 28 Justin Sullivan/Getty Images; p. 29 Joe Raedle/Getty Images; p. 31 © Steven Widoff/Alamy; p. 33 © www.istockphoto.com/Sean Locke; p. 36 © Lauren Marsh/Syracuse Newspapers/The Image Works; p. 39 Feature Photo Service/Newscom; p. 40 © AP Images; p. 44 © Bob Daemmrich/The Image Works; p. 46 © www.istockphoto.com/Gary Martin; p. 51 © Bonnie Kamin/PhotoEdit.

Designer: Sam Zavieh; Editor: Kathy Kuhtz Campbell; Photo Researcher: Amy Feinberg